CENGAGE Learning

Nonfiction Classics for Students, Volume 5

Project Editor
David Galens **Editorial**
Sara Constantakis, Anne Marie Hacht, Ira
Mark Milne, Pam Revitzer, Kathy Sauer,
Timothy J. Sisler, Jennifer Smith, Carol
Ullmann **Research**
Michelle Campbell, Sarah Genik, Tamara Nott
Permissions
Lori Hines

Manufacturing
Stacy Melson **Imaging and Multimedia**
Lezlie Light, Daniel William Newell, David G.
Oblender, Kelly A. Quin **Product Design**
Pamela A. E. Galbreath © 2003 by Gale. Gale is an
imprint of Gale,
Inc., a division of Thomson Learning Inc.

For more information, contact

Gale
27500 Drake Rd.
Farmington Hills, MI 48331-3535
Or you can visit our Internet site at
http://www.gale.com

While every effort has been made to ensure the reliability of the information presented in this

ISBN 0-7876-6034-5
ISSN 1533-7561

Printed in the United States of America
10 9 8 7 6 5 4 3 2 1

The Golden Bough

James Frazer 1890

Introduction

Ever since its first edition in 1890, *The Golden Bough* has been considered a major influence in the development of western thought. In this book, Sir James G. Frazer, a Cambridge researcher trained in classical literature, outlines ancient myths and folk legends, proposing that all civilizations go through three stages of development: belief in magic leads to organized religion, which eventually leads to faith in the powers of science. Frazer's literary style raised interest in the ideas of other world cultures at a time when western societies considered the peoples of Africa and Asia to be the products of "primitive" thought. In addition, his attempts to identify the basic story motifs to which all human beings respond was carried forth in the twentieth century by psychologists such as Carl Jung, who developed the idea of the collective unconscious, and by such literary masters as James Joyce and T. S. Eliot.

Frazer went on to expand the original book, first to a two-volume set and then to a total of thirteen volumes, before editing it down to one concise volume, which is the one that is most commonly read today. Over time, the book's reputation has changed. While it was once considered to be an important study in comparative anthropology, many social scientists later found fault with the methods that Frazer used in collecting materials: he never spoke directly to people of the cultures about which he wrote, but instead he relied on other researchers' findings and on questionnaires that he gave to people who traveled to other lands. Frazer's conclusions are generally considered unreliable because he did not follow sound scientific procedures, but *The Golden Bough* is still revered as a well-written introduction to the subject of comparative religion.

Author Biography

James George Frazer was born on January 1, 1854, in Glasgow, Scotland. As he grew up he developed an interest in classical literature, which was his major when he enrolled in Glasgow University at age fifteen. After graduating Glasgow he received a scholarship to Trinity College at Cambridge, where he was given a teaching position in 1879. For the rest of his life, except for one unsatisfying year at Liverpool University in 1907, Frazer was associated with Trinity College.

In his early years at Trinity, Frazer formed a relationship with William Robertson Smith, who at that time was assembling the ninth edition of the *Encyclopaedia Britannica*. Smith asked Frazer, who had recently become interested in the cultures and stories of primitive people, to write an article about totemism for the encyclopedia. Frazer was a dedicated writer, spending twelve and fourteen hours a day researching in the library; when his finished entry proved too long to include in the encyclopedia, he published it as his first book, *Totemism*, in 1887.

Soon after that, Frazer started on what was to be the defining work of his lifetime, *The Golden Bough: A Study in Comparative Religion*. A two-volume edition was published in 1890; it was expanded to a three-volume edition that was published in 1900. Between 1911 and 1915 a thirteen-volume edition came out. In 1922, Frazer edited the twelve books down to one abridged edition. A revised abridged edition was released thirty-seven years later, in 1959, long after his death.

Most of Frazer's other writings revolved around anthropological themes that were introduced in *The Golden Bough*. These include *The Scope of Social Anthropology* (1908); *The Worship of Nature* (1926); and *Myths of the Origin of Fire* (1930). In 1914 he was knighted in recognition of his work.

Frazer died in 1941 in Cambridge, where he taught. He is credited by many with being one of the most influential writers of the twentieth century.

Plot Summary

Chapters 1-2

The entire line of inquiry of *The Golden Bough* is developed from one particular ritualistic practice that Frazer describes in the book's early pages. In Italy, he explains, there is a wooded area on the shore of Lake Nemi, which is dedicated to the memory of the Roman goddess Diana. By tradition, each priest of Diana who guards the forest, known as the King of the Wood, gained his position by murdering the priest who held the position before him. Tradition held that the King of the Wood must be killed by an escaped slave who would beat the king to death with a golden bough taken from a tree that grew in the grove. Frazer was curious about several elements in this tradition. He wondered why the priest is referred to as a king, a practice he learned was fairly common. Next, he wondered about the probability that the priest would spend much time worrying about would-be assassins ready to take his position from him. Finally, Frazer wondered why the golden bough was so important to the ritual and why there was an assumption that the branch of gold would always be available. Frazer's search for more information generates a long inquiry into myths and beliefs of various cultures.

Chapters 3-15

For an extended section near the beginning of his inquiry, Frazer looks at concepts associated with magic and how magic evolved into religion. He shows how kings were thought to have magical powers and how that idea translated throughout the ancient world into the idea of the king as a religious figure, sometimes equated with a god. At the same time, he also explores how trees, particularly oaks, came to hold special significance in agrarian societies.

Chapters 16-28

After establishing the connection between secular rulers and religion, Frazer looks at the ways in which this relationship endangered those important personages. He discusses taboos at length, drawing from a variety of cultures to establish that taboos occur both as primitive superstitions and as beliefs in modern, cultivated societies. Once he has described forbidden acts and how they fit into the established social order, Frazer brings in examples where the forbidden actions actually become part of the social code, focusing on the taboos that limited the actions of the king and/or priest. The discussion then leads to cultures that practice the killing of kings (so that their divine powers will not be left to wither with age) and the killing of sacred trees.

Chapters 29-49

Tying in myths that are related to the story of Diana, such as those involving Adonis, Attis, Osiris, and Demeter and Persephone, Frazer shows how various deities in world religions have been connected to the agricultural cycle of life and death. Each of these myths involves an important figure who is identified with the growth cycle, a figure who dies or is stolen away to the underworld but then is allowed to return to the earth for limited stretches of time, illustrating the idea that the deaths of gods are not catastrophic, but instead are considered to be part of the process of nature.

Chapters 50-61

Frazer explores a variety of methods of sacrifice throughout time and in different lands, including ritual killing of sacred animals in order to honor gods and killing animals as a way of symbolically killing evil. This discussion presents the concept of the scapegoat, which was originally an actual goat meant to represent evil but later came to be a human being who represented evil and was killed for the same purpose. Frazer draws connections between the idea of murdering kings in order to retain their divine power while it is still at its peak and the idea of killing people who can then take evil to the grave with them, and he speculates that the two practices became joined as one.

Chapters 62-67

In theorizing about why the golden bough is so important to the tradition of succession of the King of the Wood, Frazer connects gold, the sun, fire, and power. Trees that had been hit by lightning were, for example, often seen as especially significant because they were thought to have even more fire in them than ordinary trees that were burned for fuel. Frazer speculates that the golden bough may be an ancient name for mistletoe, which grows as a vine on oak trees, turns yellow or golden while the rest of the tree remains green, and is thought in several cultures to have mystical properties. Connecting the magical power of the kings with the magical powers ascribed to mistletoe, Frazer identifies the belief that the soul of a person could be put into some object for safekeeping and the belief that important persons could only be killed by something that was already a part of them: thus, if the power of the King of the Wood was already in the mistletoe, it would make sense that the bough would be the only thing needed to kill him.

Chapters 68-69

In the last two chapters, Frazer returns to the question of why the priest of Diana must be killed and why by the particular prescribed method. One conclusion to be reached from this inquiry, he says, is that the process of civilization leads from a primitive belief in magic to a more orderly belief in religion to, ultimately, a belief in science. Though confident that this is the natural progression for any society, he reminds readers that science is not necessarily the end of human growth and that there may be other systems of belief that will supplant it in the future.

Adonis

In addition to his story being a fixture of the Greek tradition, the legend of the Greek god Adonis, also known as Tammuz, has roots stretching back to Babylonia and Syria. As both Tammuz in Babylonia and Adonis in Greece, he was a god of vegetation and was seen as the embodiment of masculine beauty. He was loved by Aphrodite, the goddess of beauty, who hid him in a gold chest, which she gave to Persephone, the queen of the underworld, for safekeeping. When Persephone peeked in the chest and saw Adonis, she was captivated with his beauty and refused to give him back to Aphrodite. Zeus settled the dispute by giving him to each goddess for part of the year. The change of seasons was explained in connection to the place where Adonis was during each part of the year, since Aphrodite, lamenting when he was gone, refused to help plants or animals grow, marking winter in climates where it did not snow.

Aeneas

Aeneas is a central figure of Roman mythology. He is the title character of Virgil's masterpiece *The Aeneid,* which recounts his seven years of travels after the Greeks' siege of Troy. His journey ended when he landed in Italy and founded

Rome. According to legend, Aeneas, before going to the underworld, was told that he must take with him a golden bough from an evergreen oak tree that grew in the grove of Diana, to give as a gift to the Queen of the Underworld.

Artemis

See Diana

Attis

Like Adonis, Attis was a god of vegetation, worshipped in Phrygia. He was a shepherd, famed for his good looks and beloved by Cybele, the goddess of fertility. His death is explained in different ways in different versions of his story, and he is said to have been turned into a pine tree, linking him to the tree mythology that drives the story of *The Golden Bough.* In a similar way to the story of Demeter and Persephone, Attis' death caused Cybele to grieve so much that the earth was thrown into a famine, and it is for this reason that annual rituals were performed in the fall to mourn the loss of Attis and in the spring to celebrate his return from the underworld.

Balder

In Scandinavian mythology, Balder the Beautiful could be harmed by nothing on heaven or earth except a bough of mistletoe. Frazer supposes that Balder was a personification of the mistletoe that grows on the oak tree, which was worshipped as sacred by the Scandinavians. This mistletoe is considered to be a possible source for the idea of the golden tree bough referred to in the book's title, thereby connecting the ancient Roman ritual practiced in Italy with the religious practices that developed in the countries of northern Europe.

Demeter

Demeter is the Greek goddess of the harvest. The story of Demeter and her daughter Persephone, one of the oldest Greek myths, has parallels in many ancient cultures. According to the myth, when Persephone was carried off by the lord of the underworld, Demeter refused to help the harvest, causing famine across the Earth. Zeus, the king of the gods, returned Persephone to her but ruled that she could only spend two-thirds of the year with Demeter and had to return to Hades for four months of the year. For the four months annually that she is gone, Demeter is said to mourn, accounting for the lack of vegetation in the wintertime. Frazer's analysis of the story centers on the poem *Hymn to Demeter,* by Homer. Elements of her story are found throughout the world, traced through the "corn-mother" goddess worshipped by Cretans during the Stone Age and similar stories about characters identified as corn spirits.

Diana

One of the most important figures in classical

mythology, Diana is the Roman goddess of the hunt and of childbirth, associated with the Greek goddess Artemis. Her association with childbirth and fertility, as well as with hunting, led to the belief that she was also the goddess of wood, and in particular of oak, which is specified in the rituals that Frazer examines in *The Golden Bough*. The temple of Diana of the Wood, near the village of Nemi in Italy, is guarded by a priest who has earned his position by killing the previous priest, a ritual on which Frazer builds the book.

Dionysus

Dionysus is the god associated with the grape and, by extension, with wine and drunkenness. A religion was formed around the worship of him, celebrating the irrational over the rational, countering the focus on reason that characterized Greek culture. He is related to the book's focal story about the golden bough because, in addition to being god of grapes, he is considered god of all trees. Moreover, the practice of sacrificing goats in ceremonies to honor Dionysus resembles the ritual sacrifice of the King of the Forest in the golden bough tradition.

Egeria

Egeria is a water-nymph who is important in the sacred grove at Nemi because, like Diana, she can give ease to women in childbirth. Sometimes Egeria is considered to be another form of Diana.

Hippolytus

See Virbius

Isis

Sister and wife of Osiris in Egyptian mythology, Isis was given dozens of different personalities throughout the years. Frazer speculates that one of her original functions in mythology was that she was thought to be the goddess of corn and barley, having discovered them and given them to mankind. Over time, her image changed from that of the plain corn-mother (a function shared by the Roman goddess Diana) to a glamorous beauty, and as this transformation occurred she grew to be the most popular of all Egyptian deities.

King of the Wood

The King of the Wood is the traditional priest of the Arician grove. Frazer recounts how this position has been handed down, generation after generation, since antiquity. The book's title, *The Golden Bough*, refers to the tradition that states that the King of the Woods must be killed by an escaped slave, hit with a golden bough from a tree that grows there. The person who kills him then becomes the new King of the Wood. He is thought to represent a worldly husband to the goddess Diana. Throughout the course of the book, Frazer speculates about various theories explaining how the king's ritual murder came to be custom. The history of the position, as well as similar rituals in other cultures, is explored. Using this particularly significant ritual, Frazer examines the implications of hundreds of beliefs and their evolution over the centuries.

Numa

Numa was a wise king who was a husband or lover of Egeria. Since the legend of Egeria is closely associated with that of Diana, Frazer speculates that Numa has a place in the cult at Nemi that serves as a basis of the book. Numa is often thought to be another form of the King of the Wood.

Osiris

Osiris is an ancient Egyptian god whose death and resurrection were celebrated each year. Osiris was the most popular of Egyptian deities, and he was worshipped for centuries. As an Egyptian king, he is credited with having taught the Egyptians how to cultivate fruit from trees, while Isis, who was both his sister and his wife, taught the people how to plant and harvest grains. Osiris traveled the world, teaching people of foreign lands how to grow crops. When he returned to Egypt, though, he was ambushed by a cadre of forty-seven conspirators, led by one of his own brothers; they tricked him into a box and, sealing the lid, sent it floating off down the Nile. Isis found his body downstream and buried it, but Osiris lived on as the lord of the underworld.

Orestes

A very famous figure in Greek mythology, Orestes is thought, according to one legend, to have started the cult of Diana of the Woods. After killing the King of the Tauric Chersonese, Orestes is said to have fled to Nemi, the place where the golden bough ritual is followed, thereby introducing Diana to that part of Italy.

Persephone

Greek myth explains how Persephone, the daughter of Demeter, was playing in a field one day and was carried off by the Lord of the Underworld, Pluto. When Demeter's grief threatened to destroy the world with famine, Zeus arranged for Persephone to return to the surface world for two-thirds of the year, but for the last third she always had to be Pluto's bride again in Hades. She also figures into the story of Adonis, with whom she fell in love and whom she tried to keep in the underworld with her, although Zeus allowed him to return to the earth's surface for several months each year to be with Aphrodite, who loved him first.

Tammuz

See Adonis

Virbius

Bearing the Roman name for the Greek hero Hippolytus, Virbius was Diana's lover and showed no interest in other women. When the goddess Aphrodite tried to take Virbius for herself he spurned her advances, and in her humiliation she persuaded his father to kill him, but Diana brought him back to life and hid him at Nemi. Among the rituals that make up the focus of *The Golden Bough*, Frazer includes the ban on horses at Nemi, which is thought to have started in recognition of the fact that Virbius was said to have been killed by being dragged behind horses. He is considered to be the founder of the sacred grove and the first king of Nemi.

Themes

Search for Knowledge

The central subject of this book, and the source of its title, is the ritual replacement of the priest of Diana at Aricia through murder. Frazer was so curious about this myth that he examined it with meticulous attention to detail. Hundreds of pages filled with thousands of examples from cultures throughout history are devoted to exploring myth. *The Golden Bough* contains sections that seem unrelated to Diana and the King of the Wood. Readers who do not follow the book from its beginning might wonder, for example, how it could possibly lead from Roman mythology to eighteenth-century Irish Christmas rituals or the custom of people of New Hebrides who throw their food leftovers into the sea.

Despite its strange and twisting side trips, though, this book returns to its main point often enough to assure readers that it is, in fact, about that one specific myth. In addressing the question with such a tidal wave of information about a variety of cultures, Frazer illustrates something about knowledge and how it is acquired. The message that is embedded in his method is that knowledge is not simple or isolated but is instead only relevant when it is connected to related facts, which are themselves related to other facts.

Search for Self

In the course of discussing one academic question that leads him to a myriad of exotic, ancient cultural traditions, Frazer ends up showing how remote practices relate to modern times. With books about psychology or contemporary life, it is easy for readers to connect to their own lives, but *The Golden Bough* is burdened with the added responsibility of subject material that its author considers important precisely because it does not seem to directly affect his life or the lives of his readers. From the very beginning of the book, he does nothing to tell readers why they should care, leaving it to their own intelligence to deduce what the practices of dead civilizations have to do with the state of humanity today. Still, the personal relevance of everything in the book is hard to miss. The cold approach that Frazer takes toward the many cultures that he mentions in this book might be seen as a way for readers to distance themselves from his subjects, but then again, it is more likely to make readers see their own lives from the outside, through the objective eyes of the scientist.

The taboos of other cultures are different, but similar in structure, to modern cultural standards. The values of hunters and farmers, so strongly based in the cycles of the moon and the seasons, regulate modern life, from the holidays of the Judeo-Christian tradition (which coincide with pagan calendars) to the nine-month schedule of the U.S. school year. The tradition of sacrificing powerful priests and kings tells readers much about the otherwise contradictory ways celebrities are treated. In all of the traditions that Frazer has included in *The Golden Bough*, there is a common thread. He emphasizes this commonality by drawing his examples from as wide a pool as possible, in order to show that his ideas are not limited to just a few societies that happen to be similar. Frazer presents enough examples to make a convincing argument that what he says applies to the basic human situation.

Topics for Further Study

- Look for a behavior that is apparent in everyday life but that people seem to do for no other reason than tradition. Try to discover what that behavior might have developed from. Another way to go about this topic is to think about the mythical history of some object that did not exist when Frazer wrote, such as computers or cars.

- Make a chart or "family tree" of the mythical figures who are mentioned in *The Golden Bough*, showing their relationship to one another.

- George Lucas has said that he based much of his *Star Wars* film saga on mythological motifs. Research which mythic stories Lucas had in mind, and find where they fit into the argument Frazer presents in *The Golden Bough*.

- Choose one of the myths mentioned in the book and make your own picture of it, the way that Turner depicted the scene at the lake of Nemi.

Archetype

An archetype is a model or type in literature that is considered to be universal, occurring in all cultures at all places and times. The story of the King of the Wood that Frazer focuses on in *The Golden Bough* has details that are specific to its context that do not appear in other circumstances, and so it cannot be considered archetypal. However, in trying to trace the source of this unique myth, Frazer finds that it derives from many other archetypes that gather together. Some examples of these are the stories of gods who bring on winter by descending to hell for several months a year; corn mother myths; ritual murder of scapegoats; and the reverence for the oak tree in societies where it grows. These archetypes are familiar, in some form, to all cultures. Some twentieth-century psychologists have speculated that archetypes are embedded in the genetic code of humans.

Folklore

The word "folklore" refers to the beliefs and traditions of groups of people. Usually, these cultural aspects are not formally recorded by the culture itself, which might be unaware of them; they are more likely to be recorded by an outside anthropologist. At the time that Frazer started to work on *The Golden Bough*, interest in the beliefs of the common people of a given culture was just starting to gain recognition: the word "folklore" was coined in 1846, just a few decades before Frazer's first edition.

Objectivity

One of the most notable aspects of Frazer's style is the dry, scientific tone of his writing. He never conveys an opinion or any feeling about the stories he relates. Given the volume of information that he presents, this objectivity can make it difficult for readers to absorb what he has to say: because the work shows no variance nor any emotional involvement of any kind, readers are left to determine the importance of each piece of information for themselves. Even though this characteristic makes the book less interesting to read, Frazer's objective tone is necessary. This book's main purpose is to be educational, not entertaining, and the objective tone assures that he is taking a properly neutral stance toward what he is reporting.

Historical Context

Frazer published the first edition of *The Golden Bough* in 1890, just eight years after the death of Charles Darwin. Darwin, a British naturalist, considered to be one of the greatest scientists of the nineteenth century, developed a theory of evolution, which he outlined in his 1859 book *On the Origins of Species.* This work popularized the phrase "survival of the fittest." According to Darwinian evolution, the species that were best fitted to their environments were the ones that were bound to survive, while the ones that were not well adapted tended to die off and become extinct. Within a species, genetic adaptations were achieved when those organisms that had the traits that were most important for their survival, such as speed or strength, were the ones that lived long enough to reproduce with other survivors, and the offspring of such unions inherited advantageous traits, making each generation more likely to mature and reproduce than the previous one.

Darwin also argued that all organisms were descended from one single source and that they changed as they adapted to different situations. This idea, developed further in 1871 in *The Descent of Man,* met with much stronger opposition than the idea of natural selection and is contested to this day by some religious fundamentalists. Still, even his detractors would be forced to admit that Darwin was one of the most influential scientists of his day.

In *The Golden Bough*, readers can get a feel for the enthusiasm that Darwin's theories inspired in scientists of the late nineteenth century. Frazer's explanation of how cultures inevitably develop from primitive belief in magic to more complex belief in religion and then, finally, to a reliance on science shows an unwavering faith in the idea that, over time, entire systems of belief evolve from one form to another. It is a supposition, like Darwin's evolutionary scale, that would have seemed impossible to an earlier generation. By the end of the nineteenth century, however, sciences had shifted their focus from examining isolated events to studying events in respect to their relationship to similar events. Like Darwin, who had studied the different adaptations in similar species that had evolved in different climates, Frazer speculated about the ways that different story motifs appeared in altered but recognizable form in different cultures.

Frazer's belief in society's inevitable growth toward faith in science—which, today, is the theory of his that is most often rejected—can be seen mirrored in the works of the most well-known economic writer of his time, Karl Marx. In his 1848 tract *The Communist Manifesto,* Marx proposed that all world governments would pass through specific, predetermined periods of growth before ending up with Communist political structures. Like Frazer, Marx believed that there was just one logical outcome to the growth of society, and he believed that he could determine it scientifically.

While his theories about cultural progression were challenged from the very first publication of *The Golden Bough*, Frazer is still acknowledged as a highly influential anthropologist. His work generated a new interest in comparative anthropology, influencing a generation of late nineteenth-century psychologists, including Sigmund Freud (whose theories often alluded to stories from ancient myths) and Carl Jung (whose theory of the collective unconscious seems to explain Frazer's ideas of universal myths). *The Golden Bough* also influenced literature, particularly the work of James Joyce and T. S. Eliot. Within its own field of anthropology, however, Frazer's work has not been very influential, owing to the fact that he did not gather his information directly from the people about whom he wrote. All of his work is based on secondhand information rather than field work, and as a result the value of his writing is considered marginal.

Critical Overview

When it was first published, *The Golden Bough* was considered an insightful work that tied together the widely divergent canon of anthropology into one cohesive theory. The book was praised for its thoroughness and accepted as a major scientific accomplishment. A 1890 review in the *Journal of American Folklore,* for instance, proclaimed the anonymous reviewer "grateful" to Frazer "for the exhibition of materials so rich, and for the literary skill with which he has made accessible observations so important to the central ideas of our modern thought." As time passed, however, questions arose about Frazer's methodology, which consisted of combining works that were gathered through non-scientific methods. His use of hearsay and third-person accounts of cultural practices made anthropologists doubt the value of his work as science.

Compare & Contrast

- **1890:** People in Europe and the United States know little about non-Western culture; they refer to Africa as "The Dark Continent" and Asia as "The Mysterious Orient."

  Today: Inexpensive travel and the Internet have made it possible for people all over the world to be aware of distant cultures.

- **1890:** Greek mythology is studied in almost all schools and is generally well-known.

  Today: More students know about the Greek gods from Disney movies than from studying them in class.

- **1890:** A scholar like Frazer can make an international reputation for his theories by making assumptions about the results of other anthropologists' work.

  Today: Leading scientists have research assistants who can assemble data under their supervision.

Still the book's reputation as a work of literature grew. It was recognized as having influenced such important twentieth-century thinkers as Freud, Anatole France, Arnold Toynbee, Margaret Mead, and Oswald Spengler. In 1941, noted anthropologist Bronislaw Malinowski noted an inconsistency in Frazer's impact on the intellectual community when he stated that "Frazer was and is one of the world's greatest teachers and masters" but that, despite his enormous following, "[h]is inability to convince seems to contradict his power to convert and to inspire." His point was that other writers followed Frazer for his vision and for the far-reaching thoroughness of his theories, even though they did not believe in the actual theories. By the second half of the century, critics found little sense in dwelling on shortcomings in *The Golden Bough* and instead accepted its impact. Stanley Edgar Hyman, for instance, wrote in 1962 that the book is "not primarily anthropology, if it ever was, but a great imaginative vision of the human condition." He saw no problem with reading this book, which was meant to be a scientific work, as a work of literature, noting that the author was trained in literature and not in anthropology: "It is in his original field of classical studies … that Frazer may have produced his greatest effect." Since then, many critics have joined Hyman in accepting *The Golden Bough* as an important piece of literature, but not as an important scientific achievement.

What Do I Read Next?

- Joseph Campbell was arguably the most popular writer on myth in the late twentieth century. His most famous work is *The Power of Myth,* an overview of how mythology is relevant to contemporary life. The book was based on a six-part series that Campbell did for Public Television with Bill Moyers. It was published in 1991 by Anchor.

- Readers who are interested in Frazer's historical place as a student of myths can find out the state of the discipline before him in *The Rise of Modern Mythology, 1680-1860.* In this 1972 volume, authors Burton Feldman and Robert D. Richards give biographies of and samples from the great writers about myth, from Bernard Fontenelle (1657-1757) to Henry David Thoreau (1817-1862).

- In *Myth: Its Meaning and Function,* G. S. Kirk deals with weaknesses he found in works by Frazer and his followers: those of examining myths in relation to folktales and to rituals. This book was published by Cambridge University in 1970.

- *Schrödinger's Cat and "The Golden Bough"* (2000), by physicist Randy Bancroft, attempts to tie together science, magic, and mythology for the modern reader. It was published by University Press of America.

Sources

Hyman, Stanley Edgar, "What Do You Dance?," in *The Tangled Bank: Darwin, Marx, Frazer, and Freud as Imaginative Writers,* Atheneum, 1962, pp. 212-32.

Malinowski, Bronislaw, "Sir James George Frazer," in *A Scientific Theory of Culture and Other Essays,* University of North Carolina Press, 1944, pp. 177-221.

Review of *The Golden Bough,* in the *Journal of American Folklore,* Vol. 3, No. 40, October—December 1890, pp. 316-9.

Further Reading

Bruner, Jerome S., "Myth and Identity," in *Myth and Mythmaking,* edited by Henry A. Murray, Beacon Press, 1960, pp. 276-87.

> Bruner examines the psychological reasons why humans are attracted to myths.

Downie, R. Angus, *Frazer and "The Golden Bough,"* Victor Gollancz Ltd., 1970.

> This study examines Frazer's entire career, including his influences, his methods, and his other writings.

Patai, Raphael, *Myth and Modern Man,* Prentice-Hall, Inc., 1972.

> Patai, whose early career interests overlapped with Frazer's, examines mythological aspects in contemporary America in such chapters as "Madison Avenue Myth and Magic," "The Myth of Oral Gratification: Coke and Smoke," and "The New Sex Myth."

Vickery, John B. *The Literary Impact of "The Golden Bough,"* Princeton University Press, 1973.

> The focus here is on works by Yeats, D. H. Lawrence, T. S. Eliot, and James Joyce, all of which show

Frazer's influence. Nearly a quarter
of the book is about James Joyce.

Milton Keynes UK
Ingram Content Group UK Ltd.
UKHW020723120224
437701UK00018B/620